THE
WILDERNESS
EXPERIENCE

ECHOES FROM THE SUMMIT

WRITINGS AND PHOTOGRAPHS

SELECTED AND EDITED BY

PAUL SCHULLERY

A Harvest Original

HARCOURT BRACE & COMPANY

SAN DIEGO • NEW YORK • LONDON

A TEHABI BOOK

Requests for permission to make copies of any part of the work should be mailed to: Permissions Department, Harcourt Brace & Company, 6277 Sea Harbor Drive, Orlando, Florida 32887-6777.

Rick Bass, excerpt from *Wild to the Heart* by Rick Bass. Copyright © 1987 by Rick Bass. Reprinted by permission of Stackpole Books.

Harry Middleton, excerpt from *On the Spine of Time* by Harry Middleton. Copyright © 1991 by Harry Middleton. Reprinted with permission in its abridged form by IMG Julian Bach Literary Agency, Inc.

John Muir, excerpt from "A Near View of the High Sierra" by John Muir. Copyright © 1894. Excerpted from *John Muir, The Mountains of California*, 1988, Dorset Press (Barnes & Noble).

Sigurd F. Olson, from *Runes of the North* by Sigurd F. Olson. Copyright © 1963 by Sigurd F. Olson. Reprinted by permission of Alfred A. Knopf, Inc.

Doug Peacock, excerpts from *The Wind Rivers* by Doug Peacock. Published in *Northern Lights*, Vintage Books, 1994. Used with permission of author in its abridged form.

Ruth Rudner, *Greetings From Wisdom, Montana*, by Ruth Rudner. Copyright © 1989. Reprinted with permission in its abridged form by Fulcrum Publishing, Golden, Colorado. 800-992-2908.

Henry David Thoreau, excerpt "Ktaadn" from *The Maine Woods*, Boston, Ticknor and Fields, 1864.

Library of Congress Cataloging-in-Publication Data
Echoes from the summit: writings and photographs / selected and edited by Paul Schullery. — 1st ed.
     p.   cm.— (The wilderness experience)
"A Harvest original."
"A Tehabi book."
   ISBN 0-15-600228-0 (pbk.)
   1. Natural history—United States. 2. Mountains—United States. 3. United States—Description and travel.
4. Natural history—United States—Pictorial works. 5. Mountains—United States—Pictorial works. 6. United States—Pictorial works.
I. Schullery, Paul. II. Series.
QH104.E36 1996
508.73—dc20

96-13547
CIP

Echoes from the Summit was conceived and produced by Tehabi Books. Nancy Cash–*Series Editor and Developmental Editor*; Laura Georgakakos–*Manuscript Editor;* Kathi George-*Copy Proofer;* Andy Lewis–*Art Director;* Sam Lewis–*Art Director;* Tom Lewis–*Editorial and Design Director;* Sharon Lewis–*Controller;* Chris Capen–*President.*

Harcourt Brace & Company and Tehabi Books, in association with The Basic Foundation, a not-for-profit organization whose primary mission is reforestation, will facilitate the planting of two trees for every one tree used in the manufacture of this book. This edition is printed on acid-free paper that meets the American National Standards Institute Z39.48 Standard.

Printed in Hong Kong through Mandarin Offset.
First edition 1996
A B C D E

CONTENTS

ECHOES FROM THE SUMMIT

We are blessed with mountains. I can't imagine living in a country without them. Whether I am hauling my grouse gun up some rounded old New England peak, exploring some redrock mesa in the Four Corners Country, or drifting a fly through a likely stretch on a high-Sierra brook, I feel the peculiar power of the uplands.

At the same time, I'm reminded of our enduring relationship with these places. In some unlikely, bramble-ledged hollow on that New England mountain I suddenly come upon a century-old stone fence and a few ancient apple trees, where once a family made this slope their own, then gave it back to the forest. Everywhere in the Southwest, pre-Columbian human habitations are carved into the redrock, standing in tilting weathered walls, or buried under shallow soil mounds. And when a trout takes my fly at 9,000 feet in the Sierra, it's a nonnative brook trout brought to this water in the 1800s by restless nonnative people for whom the native fish were not enough.

We are likewise blessed with mountain writers. As long as I've been old enough to travel these places, I've loved sharing them with earlier visitors who took the trouble to write down how it all felt to them. The literature of mountains, a huge, diffuse body of adventure, reflection, and wisdom, is a national treasure no less than are the mountains themselves. It is distinguished from most other topical literatures by its scattered sources. Whether you read textbooks of ecology and geology, the adventure writings of hunters and fishermen, the conservation tracts of our great professional resource managers, the harrowing, cliff-hugging accounts of the technical climbers, the passionate essays of our naturalists, or the personal reminiscences of countless other mountain people—ranchers, rangers, storekeepers, and no end of drifters, part-timers, river-rats, and hermits—you are likely to run into the praise of high country.

Has there ever been a human culture not intrigued with high places? Any time our landscape climbs, be it a low ridge on the prairie or a horizon-splitting peak, we are attracted to the top, even if we only look and wonder what it's like up there. For as long as humans have had even a spark of wonder in our souls, we have sought these places for solitude, for inspiration, for vision, and just for this vague urge we have, to get the best possible view.

That vague urge may be the most interesting impulse of all. It takes little imagination to wonder if our desire to see things from the top isn't a leftover behavioral trait from the Pleistocene, when we shared the world with predators who were faster and stronger than we, and only our ability to understand our world gave us an edge. In that world, high places were both refuge and lookout: the best spots from which to keep watch, for both our predators and the prey we shared.

The road from that hilltop to modern mountain appreciation is a long and complicated one. It's easy to see the immense pyramids of both the Old and New World as artificial hills, which they were: ceremonial eminences that emphasized the power, even the otherworldliness, of whoever ran the temples on top. This is easy for me to appreciate. Whenever I visit any of the remaining moundbuilder sites scattered up and down the Mississippi Valley, I'm disappointed if the regulations forbid me from climbing to the top of these thousand-year-old monuments. I don't know what I expect to gain from getting up there, but I know it's the right place to be.

We have never stopped redefining our mountains, and at times the pursuit of understanding has become fairly esoteric. In seventeenth-century England, for example, debates raged over what mountains should mean to enlightened people. One school of thought held that they were "frightful disfigurements" and "unnatural protuberances upon the face of the earth." Adherents to this position tended to believe that the world had been created "perfect," that is, egg-smooth, but was ruined and scarred by the Biblical deluge. But even back then, when any form of wilderness was generally thought of as dangerous and evil, another much more positive view held that mountains were in fact "the turnings and carvings and ornamental sculptures that make up the lineaments of nature." Nature, this view held, could be terrible and beautiful at the same time; these folks were far from the first to notice that when you stood on top of a mountain you were in fact just that much closer to Heaven. They don't call it higher ground for nothing.

Citizens of today's interwoven global culture have inherited these views, and many more, and if you look hard enough you will certainly find traces of them in the selections in this book. But modern mountain appreciation goes far beyond arguing if mountains are good or bad. As this collection shows, mountains are to be taken personally, and we are all left to find our own way in the high country.

What I find especially intriguing in these selections is that the mountain continues to be a stage for the drama of human life. For all our awe at their sheer size—Theodore Roosevelt celebrated the "stupendous mountain masses" of the Rockies—we spend most of our time in the literary high country talking about ourselves. Mountains represent a way of life, and a way to relate ourselves to our world.

We go to the mountains as much to be *in* them as to be *on* them. Harry Middleton's tales of his many pilgrimages to the coves and trout streams of the southern Appalachians were almost without mention of peaks or summits, but in the high, secluded valleys of the great southeastern mountain ranges, he found life—his own, and those of the people he met—better. Mountain life revitalized him, putting him through some kind of purification process that clarified everything.

Like so many earlier generations, many of the writers in this collection also find that mountain life has spiritual values. Thoreau invoked mythology on these "sacred and mysterious tracts," while Muir depended upon some indefinable "other self, bygone experiences, Instinct, or Guardian Angel" to allow him to reach "the topmost crag in the blessed light." Bass invokes "magic" to help him explain his mountains, while Spragg proclaims that "the higher the home, the less we are body, the more we are spirit." All of us take the mountain and connect our lives to it by these spiritual lines; we may not know where Heaven is, but we know what it looks like (a wise old fisherman I know describes his favorite high country stream as the kind of river you'd expect to find in Heaven, or be willing to go elsewhere in search of). And so it seems that we are not only blessed with mountains, we are blessed by them.

We can be too romantic about this; for all our love of them, mountains don't take a personal interest in *us*. Recently, a wise, much-traveled friend of mine, while reflecting on a climbing accident that almost cost a young man we both cared a great deal about his life, said, "Mountains don't care, Paul. I mean, they're wonderful and beautiful and everything, but they just don't care." It was a little jarring to have mountains described so coldly, but I had to admit he was right; all the caring, all the attachments and emotion, are ours. It's up to us to make what we can of mountain life. The remote, oblivious position that the mountain takes is probably one of the most important things in the process. If mountains were easier, or somehow more forgiving (willing to give us a second try if we slip, or a small loan if we run out of cash in the middle of a trip), the whole mountain world would be devalued, and a lot of us would lose interest anyway.

So my coauthors and I invite you on this tour of some personal mountains. Your guides come from many places, over many times. Their voices are remarkably dissimilar, but their passion for what the songwriter has called "life in a chosen country" is a vital part of the long tradition of human affection for our world's eminences. Whether the writer asks you to settle in for the winter in a high-meadow cabin or come along on a trek to the highest horizon, it will be a good trip with good company and all the best views. —*Paul Schullery* ❧

A GRAND AND DESOLATE PLACE

American nature writing did not begin with Henry David Thoreau, but his influence on the literature of New England has been astonishing. Reading "Ktaadn," I am reminded of why we feel compelled to call him back again and again. The very first sentence captures the mood of every hill, ridge, or mountain I've climbed, "almost as if retreating from us." Thoreau is like the first great photographer to make pictures of any grand panorama: all artists who attempt to portray the same scene must measure their work against his. —P. S.

Excerpts from *Ktaadn* by

HENRY DAVID THOREAU

At length we reached an elevation sufficiently bare to afford a view of the summit, still distant and blue, almost as if retreating from us. A torrent, which proved to be the same we had crossed, was seen tumbling down in front, literally from out of the clouds. But this glimpse at our whereabouts was soon lost, and we were buried in the woods again. The wood was chiefly yellow birch, spruce, fir, mountain-ash, or round-wood, as the Maine people call it, and moose-wood. It was the worst kind of travelling; sometimes like the densest scrub-oak patches with us. The cornel, or bunch-berries, were very abundant, as well as Solomon's seal and moose-berries. Blueberries were distributed along our whole route; and in one place bushes were drooping with the weight of the fruit, still as fresh as ever. It was the 7th of September. Such patches afforded a grateful repast, and served to bait the tired party forward. When any lagged behind, the cry of "blueberries" was most effectual to bring them up. Even at this elevation we passed through a moose-yard, formed by a large flat rock, four or five rods square, where they tread down the snow in winter. At length, fearing that if we held the direct course to the summit we should not find any water near our camping-ground, we gradually swerved to the west, till, at four o'clock, we struck again the torrent which I have mentioned, and here, in view of the summit, the weary party decided to camp that night.

While my companions were seeking a suitable spot for this purpose, I improved the little daylight that was left, in climbing the mountain alone. We were in a deep and narrow ravine, sloping up to the clouds, at an angle of nearly forty-five degrees, and hemmed in by walls of rock, which were at first covered with low trees, then with impenetrable thickets of scraggy birches and spruce-trees, and with moss, but at last bare of all vegetation but lichens, and almost continually draped in clouds. Following up the course of the torrent which occupied this—and I mean to lay some emphasis on this word *up*— pulling myself up by the side of perpendicular falls of twenty or thirty feet, by the roots of firs and birches, and then, perhaps, walking a level rod or two in the thin stream, for it took up the whole road, ascending by huge steps, as it were, a giant's stairway, down which a river flowed, I had soon cleared the trees, and paused on the successive shelves, to look back over the country. The torrent was from fifteen to thirty feet wide, without a tributary, and seemingly not diminishing in breadth as I advanced; but still it came rushing and roaring down, with a copious tide, over and amidst masses of bare rock, from the very clouds, as though a waterspout had just burst over the mountain. Leaving this at last, I began to work my way, scarcely less arduous than Satan's anciently through Chaos,[1] up the nearest, though not the highest peak. At first scrambling on all fours over the tops of ancient black spruce-trees *(Abies nigra)*, old as the flood, from two to ten or twelve feet in height, their tops flat and spreading, and their foliage blue, and nipt with cold, as if for centuries they had ceased growing upward against the bleak sky, the solid cold. I walked some good rods erect upon the tops of these trees, which were over- grown with moss and mountain-cranberries. It seemed that in the course of time they had filled up the intervals between the huge rocks, and the cold wind had uniformly levelled all over. Here the principle of vegetation was hard put to it. There was apparently a belt of this kind running quite round the mountain, though, perhaps, nowhere so remarkable as here. Once, slumping through, I looked down ten feet, into a dark and cavernous region, and saw the stem of a spruce, on whose top I stood, as on a mass of coarse basket-work, fully nine inches in diameter at the ground. These holes were bears' dens, and the bears were even then at home. This was the sort of garden I made my way *over*, for an eighth of a mile, at the risk, it is true, of treading on some of the plants, not seeing any path *through* it—certainly the most treacherous and porous country I ever travelled.

> Nigh founded on he fares,
>
> Treading the crude consistence, half on foot,
>
> Half flying.[2]

But nothing could exceed the toughness of the twigs—not one snapped under my weight, for they had slowly grown. Having slumped, scrambled, rolled, bounced, and walked, by turns, over this scraggy country, I arrived upon a sidehill, or rather side-mountain, where rocks, gray, silent rocks, were the flocks and herds that pastured, chewing a rocky cud at sunset. They looked at me with hard gray eyes, without a bleat or a low. This brought me to the skirt of a cloud, and bounded my walk that night. But I had already seen that Maine country when I turned about, waving, flowing, rippling, down below.

When I returned to my companions, they had selected a camping-ground on the torrent's edge, and were resting on the ground; one was on the sick list, rolled in a blanket, on a damp shelf of rock. It was savage and dreary scenery enough; so widly rough, that they looked long to find a level and open space for the tent. We could not well camp higher, for want of fuel; and the trees here seemed so evergreen and sappy, that we almost doubted if they would acknowledge the influence of fire; but fire prevailed at last, and blazed here too, like a good citizen of the world. Even at this height we met with frequent traces of moose, as well as of bears. As here was no cedar, we made our bed of coarser feathered spruce; but at any rate the feathers were plucked from the live tree. It was, perhaps, even a more grand and desolate place for a night's lodging than the summit would have been, being in the neighborhood of those wild trees, and of the torrent. Some more aerial and finer-spirited winds rushed and roared through the ravine all night, from time to time arousing our fire, and dispersing the embers about. It was as if we lay in the very nest of a young whirlwind. At midnight, one of my bedfellows, being startled in his dreams by the sudden blazing up to its top of a fir-tree, whose green boughs were dried by the heat, sprang up, with a cry, from his bed, thinking the world on fire, and drew the whole camp after him.

In the morning, after whetting our appetite on some raw pork, a wafer of hard bread, and a dipper of condensed cloud or waterspout, we all together began to make our way up the falls, which I have described; this time choosing the right hand, or highest peak, which was not the one I had approached before. But soon my companions were lost to my sight behind the mountain ridge in my rear, which still seemed ever retreating before me, and I climbed alone over huge rocks, loosely poised, a mile or more, still edging toward the clouds; for though the day was clear elsewhere, the summit was concealed by mist. The mountain seemed a vast aggregation of loose rocks, as if some time it had rained rocks, and they lay as they fell on the mountain sides, nowhere fairly at rest, but leaning on each other, all rocking-stones, with cavities between, but scarcely any soil or smoother shelf. They were the raw materials of a planet dropped from an unseen quarry, which the vast chemistry of nature would anon work up, or work down, into the smiling and verdant plains and valleys of earth. This was an undone extremity of the globe; as in lignite, we see coal in the process of formation.

At length I entered within the skirts of the cloud which seemed forever drifting over the summit, and yet would never be gone, but was generated out of that pure air as fast as it flowed away; and when, a quarter of a mile farther, I reached the summit of the ridge, which those who have seen in clearer weather say is about five miles long, and contains a thousand acres of table-land, I was deep within the hostile ranks of clouds, and all objects were obscured by them. Now the wind would blow me a yard of clear sunlight, wherein I stood; then a gray, dawning light was all it could accomplish, the cloud-line ever rising and falling with the wind's intensity. Sometimes it seemed as if the summit would be cleared in a few moments, and smile in sunshine; but what was gained on one side was lost on another. It was like sitting in a chimney and waiting for the smoke to blow away. It was, in fact, a cloud-factory—these were the cloud-works, and the wind turned them off done from the cool, bare rocks. Occasionally, when the windy columns broke in to me, I caught sight of a dark, damp crag to the right or left; the mist driving ceaselessly between it and me. It reminded me of the creations of the old epic and dramatic poets, of Atlas, Vulcan, the Cyclops, and Prometheus. Such was Caucasus and the rock where Prometheus was bound. Aeschylus had no doubt visited such scenery as this. It was vast, Titanic, and such as man never inhabits. Some part of the beholder, even some vital part, seems to escape through the loose grating of his ribs as he ascends. He is more lone than you can imagine. There is less of substantial thought and fair understanding in him, than in the plains where men inhabit. His reason is dispersed and shadowy, more thin and subtile, like the air. Vast, Titanic, inhuman Nature has got him at disadvantage, caught him alone, and pilfers him of some of his divine faculty. She does not smile on him as in the plains. She seems to say sternly, why came ye here before your time? This ground is not prepared for you. Is it not enough that I smile in the valleys? I have never made this soil for thy feet, this air for thy breathing, these rocks for thy neighbors, I cannot pity nor fondle thee here, but forever relentlessly drive thee hence to where I *am* kind. Why seek me where I have not called thee, and then complain because you find me but a stepmother? Shouldst thou freeze or starve, or shudder thy life away, here is no shrine, nor altar, nor any access to my ear.

> Chaos and ancient Night, I come no spy
>
> With purpose to explore or to disturb
>
> The secrets of your realm, but . . .
>
> > . . . as my way
>
> Lies through your spacious empire up to light.[3]

The tops of mountains are among the unfinished parts of the globe, whither it is a slight insult to the gods to climb and pry into their secrets, and try their effect on our humanity. Only daring and insolent men, perchance, go there. Simple races, as savages, do not climb mountains—their tops are sacred and mysterious tracts never visited by them. . . . ❧

[1] See Milton, *Paradise Lost*, II, ll. 871 ff. [2] Ibid. ll. 940–42. [3] Ibid. II, ll. 970–74.

MOUNTAIN SECRETS

Modern mountain enthusiasts are haunted by the consequences of their passion for wild country. As Rick Bass, widely acclaimed author of a series of books on nature and mountain life, suggests in this story, the last wild mountains can only stand so much love; we try to be generous, but we really want these places to ourselves. But, as Bass also shows, the urge to share—to say "look at this, it is magical and priceless"—is very strong. One of the great joys of time in the high country is sharing it with someone, and if you can't take someone along, you can tell them about it later.—P. S.

From *Wild to the Heart* by
RICK BASS

I'm going to tell you about some mountains in northern Utah.

But first, you've got to promise never to visit them. They're my mountains; I adopted them. They are the most majestic mountains in America: the wildest, freest, coldest, oldest, windiest, mountain wildflowerest, mule deerest mountains there are.

Fittingly, they run north-south, the way other North American mountain ranges run. To the north lies a great green sprawl of northern coniferous forests, and beyond that the haze of Wyoming wheatgrass prairie. Beyond that, a few more insignificant rocks, rivers, and mountains such as the Tetons, the Snake and the Yellowstone, and beyond that, Canada.

The closer you get to Canada, the more things'll eat your horse.

I tell you what—I'll do this. I'll tell you how to get to these mountains if you promise not to ever go up there while I'm visiting them. I live in Mississippi, wretched Mississippi (the "M" stands for "Mosquitoes"), and I only get up there three times a year. They are a huge mountain range; with work, there is room for both of us. I drive an orange Volkswagen Rabbit. If you see it parked by the side of the road, keep moving and don't look back. Pretend you never saw it. Natty Bumpo says git.

Except that sometimes I do this: in times of financial liberty, I fly into Salt Lake City (coach fare) and rent a car (subcompact) and drive into the mountains in the little red rent-a-car. Sometimes it is blue, though. Once it was yellow.

I pick the brightly colored little rent-cars because they stand out so well against the violet sky once I get above tree line, once I get up into the tundra and alpine meadows above 12,500 feet.

So I will do this: so that you will know it is my car, so that you can steer plenty clear of me, I'll put a pretty fair-sized rock on the hood of the car. A rock that you cannot help but see. It will be like an old Indian signal, like a trail sign: Do Not Enter.

I'll put an old rag under the rock so it doesn't scratch the paint.

Now I'll tell you about my adopted mountains. They cover many thousands of square miles, and have places in them with names like this: Moon Lake, Laughing Coyote Uplift. Wolf Tooth Creek, Spirit Lake, and the Lost Elk Caves. Lake of the Gods, and the Screaming River. Blue Hole. Lolo Pass.

Lolo Pass is, I suppose, as good a place as any to fall in love with someone.

Thunderstorms are spectacular and beautiful up in the jagged rocky peaks. They get about two per year.

They are the oldest mountains our country has; if we—and I'm considering getting a bill started in Congress—ever decided to have a National Mountain Range, this would have to be them. They're Precambrian, before Life; they've almost always been here.

Also, there's lots of bald eagles. Hiking down a narrow rushing stream, sometimes you spook them up out of dead trees. They fly off with great strong wingbeats. It is really something you should see, the way they fly.

There are a lot of dead trees up high in this mountain range. Big, dead trees, as if size and strength and age are no insurance against the winters.

I am presently trying to learn to use understatement in my writings. I believe this is a good point to practice.

Winters are harsh.

The only way into these mountains is through one of two roads. One gravelly frost-heaved road gingerly and innocently skates its way up through the western quarter of the range, going (most of the time) north-south. The other one delicately skirts the northern boundaries.

It too, is a two-laner. It's a bad place to have a busted water hose, a bad place to have a flat. There are no gas stations, there are no cafés. There is nothing that is not beautiful.

I've been up there and been snowed on in July, and August. Snowed on hard.

The two little skeins of roads that lead into the area usually close up in early November, but sometimes late October. The area sleeps undisturbed, protected under a sheet of snow and ice for as many as seven to eight months each year. It seems to me that all this ice and snow and beauty sleep preserves it, and resculpts it a little, and makes it a little more awesome each spring.

Except that spring sometimes does not come until the Fourth of July.

And yes, it does have glaciers.

It is mind-boggling to pick up a slab of rock and find in it an ancient brachiopod, a fossil of one of the earliest, most primitive sea creatures ever known, and realize that these mountains in the heartland of the United States of America were once a coastline.

Sometimes, it really makes me quite dizzy.

There's got to be a strange and long-lost history about the place; sometimes, working my way through a narrow niche in a sheer cliff wall between two wild and empty valleys, threading my way down a talus slope as a snow-dusting August storm comes rolling in low and foggy, rolling in to meet me, then sometimes I will begin crying for no reason. A terrible sadness wrenches from me, and I have to get away from the place and down to one of the meadows below me before the feeling is gone.

Other times, I start to laugh almost uncontrollably. I lean back against a tree in one of the forests and feel the rough hard texture of the bark pressing against my back and the warm forest pine straw beneath me, and for many minutes the woods will roar with great hearty booming laughs: my laughs. Laughs the likes of which Jackson, Mississippi, has never heard.

They are magic mountains.

You would not believe the alpenglow in the evenings.

The sunrises are pretty neat too.

Once, while hiking down a dark and narrow corridor of a game trail, with dense tall sweet-smelling Doug Firs and blue spruce on either side, and little blue mountain primroses for a carpet beneath me, I looked up to see someone standing in the trail ahead of me. In the shadows. It was just a silhouette.

Only it wasn't a someone; it was a doe mule deer. I stopped, and then walked closer. She did not run.

I got to within thirty or forty yards of her before she turned and ran down the trail.

I do believe it was the first time she had ever seen a human.

* * *

There are lots of good things about these mountains, but the best are the lakes.

There are lots of lakes.

Little lost slipper-sized things, they are cold and blue and clear and have lily pads around the shore and lots of fish in them.

The fish are quite tasty. The water is delicious. In November, when snow clouds come rolling in in the mornings, you can sit down on the shoreline, crouched behind a boulder or a tree, and see ducks, mallards mostly, come whistling in to splash down on the lakes.

From September to April there is ice on the ponds. Halloween weekends are the best: they are almost always frozen over by then, with a good smooth soft white blanket of snow to boot, and it is fun to go tramp words out in the middle of one of the little lens-shaped lakes. There is just one after the other after the other—they lie in chains, one- to ten-acre depressions in the glacial slickrock, usually at the base of steep cirques and cliffs.

I once spent two weeks in the summer traveling from lake to lake, fishing with spoons and spinners. I came out of the woods on the east end of the range sunburned, bearded, and twenty pounds heavier, and still I had not resolved which way I liked Utah trout best: broiled on a hot flat rock, or deep fried in bacon grease for breakfast. Toward the end of the trip I ran out of bacon grease; it was a shame too, because I had almost been ready to make my decision.

It is clear to me that my only option is to go back and try it again. Start from scratch. I will bring more bacon grease this time.

I mentioned that these are magic mountains. They are. The rocks are magic, the lakes are magic, the wind and snow and trees are magic . . . they will all talk to you, if you listen right.

A farm boy from Indiana, of all places, taught me to listen. He was a friend of Ken's and mine, my first year up at school, up at Utah State. I had applied to U.S.U. because it was the campus closest to the mountains I had seen in the movie *Jeremiah Johnson*.

He had applied to U.S.U. because once he had gone fishing for an afternoon in one of the little mountain lakes while driving cross-country through the area with his cousin. Surely you will agree with me that it takes a great deal of magic to do that, to make a farm boy from Indiana and a city boy from Texas apply to a school 2,000 miles away from home just because of a one-day fishing trip and a two-hour movie, respectively.

Once they get into you, they are as jealous as a lover; they will never let you look at other mountains again, and you will never want to.

When you are away from them, they will be all you think about. Weeks, months, even years will be measured in terms of how long you've been away, and how long it is till you return.

Now you see why I am hesitant to give you their name. Their beauty is a curse as well as a blessing. No one ever forgets them. ⚜

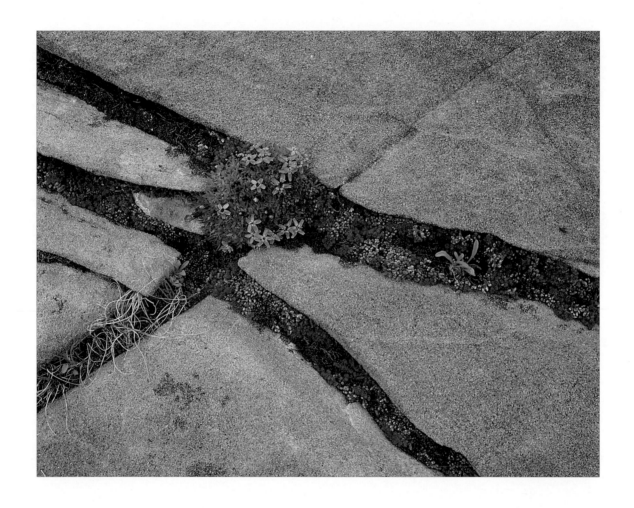

TRIAL ON THE MOUNTAIN

Doug Peacock is as firmly a part of the folklore of the western mountains as any adventurer in earlier times, and few in previous generations can match his hard-earned, colorful reputation as a risk-taker. He is known to most people as the model for Hayduke, the belligerent wilderness defender in Edward Abbey's classic environmentalist novel The Monkey Wrench Gang, *but he long ago achieved fame as a sort of underground antihero in the world of grizzly bears too. (I never read his stories without thinking that for the sake of people not so familiar with wild country, there should be a little sticker every few pages saying "Don't try this at home.") In this tale, he deals with his own recklessness in the unforgiving Wind River Range of western Wyoming. —P. S.*

Excerpts from *The Wind Rivers* by

DOUG PEACOCK

Maybe what I needed was a long infusion of solitary living. I didn't seem much good around people. The snows were melting in the high country. The bears had emerged from their winter dens. The geese had long ago flown north. If anything, I was behind schedule according to the timetable felt in my bones. Something was drawing me north, back into the land of the road map. I packed all my gear and said good-bye. I piled into the blue Jeep and headed toward the northern Rockies. . . .

I reached Wyoming in late May and spent another month watching the snow line retreat up the mountains, fishing the Popo Agie and camping out in the foothills near the Wind River Reservation. Just as summer reached the valleys, spring came to the mountains. I got ready for a long expedition into the high country, carefully packing my backpack, sorting out food and cold weather gear.

I drove the Jeep up a faint muddy track leading high into the range and left it parked in a grove of pines. I shouldered the big pack full of heavy, inexpensive gear, and headed up the trail.

The Wind River area of northwest Wyoming was considered one of the wildest spots left in the Lower Forty-eight. In 1968 the only topographical map I could find was the old Fremont version made in 1906. The area was so rugged that the surveyors had to guess at much of the country. They missed lakes and valleys and even had rivers running the wrong way, all of which let me imagine I was going somewhere unexplored and uncharted. It did not bother me that I did not know where I was going.

The first day out the weather held, and I hiked about a dozen miles, not bad considering that I had been wading through miles of creek bottom flooded by beaver dams. I made camp on the shoulder of a plateau that overlooked a long glacial valley running north. Heavy clouds gathered on the southern horizon, but I guessed that the weather would hold through the night. Just in case, I tied an army poncho corner to corner across the top of the hammock in which I would throw my sleeping bag; it was an old jungle arrangement.

The next morning broke gray and cold. Clouds blocked the passes, and the weather looked as if it would get worse. I shouldered the pack and started down the trail toward the head of a long glacial lake with a logjam across its outlet. I would cross the creek there.

By the time I got to the bottom, the clouds were rolling in and the temperature had dropped twenty degrees. I was in for a spring storm sometime that day or the next. I dug out my compass and took a reading. According to the map, that bearing should bring me to the foot of a large lake by nightfall.

By later afternoon, a wet snow had begun to fall. I slogged along through sparse timber and outcroppings of granite. By early evening a couple of inches of slush lay on the ground. I kept on the compass bearing, aiming for the large lake, which lay not more than a mile or two away. I was wet, tired of bushwhacking, and eager to set up for the night. Just at dark I stopped at an outcrop. Through the trees I could make out the slate gray surface of a large glacial lake. The wind had picked up and was blowing snowflakes into my face. It was snowing hard. I quickly put up a small mountain tent and unrolled my sleeping bag inside. I got out of my wet clothes and put on a pair of black pajama bottoms and a dry T-shirt and crawled into the sleeping bag, listening to the sound of the blizzard slapping against the tent.

I was thirsty and remembered that I had forgotten to fill my canteen. I looked out the tent flap. All I could see was the first ten feet of swirling snow. "What the hell, it will only take a minute." I stumbled down the rocky ledges toward the lake, which was probably a couple of hundred feet away. The cold wind and snow stung my arms. I pushed through a fringe of fir trees and stepped to the shore, watching the whirling snow disappear into the grayness of the mountain lake. I squatted and filled the canteen. I screwed the cap back on and turned toward my tent, shivering slightly in the cold air. I followed my tracks in the snow back through the trees. When I got to the first ledge the tracks disappeared; the blowing snow had covered them up. I could see for only a couple of feet. I did not know where my tent was.

I told myself to calm down. The tent had to be within a hundred yards or so; it was up on a bluff above the lake. Although I was almost naked, it was not dangerously cold. Dressed as I was, I might freeze if exposed to the elements for an entire night, but I still had lots of time. Methodically I began going back and forth across a series of gentle ledges, upon one of which my tent was pitched. It was so dark by then that I could barely see my feet through the falling snow. I forced myself to go ten more feet up the slope and started a new traverse.

I kept at it for about half an hour. By then I was truly cold and wanted to give up. Suddenly I tripped, falling flat on my face in the snow. I felt a guy line. I had fallen over my tent in the dark. My fingers were numb, and I clawed at the tent flap. I crawled in the entrance and stripped off my wet, frozen clothing. I zipped the sleeping bag up over my ears and pulled a woolen cap out of my clothing bag. My mind emptied, and the war marched in. . . .

In the mountains of the Wind River Range, I lay there in the tent a long time without thinking, letting the blood recirculate. It had been an altogether avoidable close call and uncharacteristically careless of me. What had happened to my concentration, to my survival instincts? This little mishap was one of several times in the previous year that I had mindlessly nearly killed myself. During the last few months I was in Vietnam I had stopped taking careful cover during firefights—I had waltzed around during gun battles like a Sioux ghost dancer, invincible against enemy bullets. I had blamed this more on weariness than on a conscious choice to take chances. But now I was forced to admit that I was truly a danger to myself. The capriciousness of survival, that random slice that separates the living from the dead, seemed like a bad joke.

"The hell with it," I said. "I've got too much to look forward to." No wacko death wish was going to get me. There were too many wild places left to explore. Besides, I liked fishing, wild mushrooms, my own cooking, Mozart, good wine, woods, and women.

I slept until the drip of water on the tent told me that the snow was melting. Around noon, I sat up and rolled out of the bag and into a gray spring day. I crammed my wet gear into the pack and broke camp. Above the lake on the far shore, timbered wedges and rotten talus swept up to unnamed peaks penetrating the glaciers that blanketed the east side of the divide. I followed the big lake to its head, where a creek dumped into the milky glacial waters. I would follow it up to a chain of small lakes, where I wanted to set up a base camp from which I could fish and explore.

The snow had melted by the time I began bushwhacking up the rocky creek bottom. I did not expect more snow, although it could have rained at any time; the weather in the Wind River Range was fickle at best. I picked up a game trail running up the drainage. In the mud there were tracks of deer, elk, and a moose. Overhanging branches slapped me in the face. No matter: I was not in a hurry.

About midafternoon I arrived at another large lake, which, according to the map, stood at the junction of two or more strings of glacial lakes. I decided to go up the longer chain, the one leading into the heart of the mountain range.

I circled the shore of the lake and lost the game trail but found the going easy enough. A heavy cloud bank hung on the crest of the range and spilled east over into my chain of lakes. Somewhere off to the west thunder rolled. The sparse lodgepole forest gave way to stunted fir and spruce mixed with five-needle pines, limber, and whitebark, indicating that I was nearing the upper limit of the trees.

Again the rumble of thunder echoed throughout the peaks and basins. I ducked into a clump of trees to wait out the passing storm—a few drops of rain with a dozen cracks of lightning. I reached the end of the lake and climbed up the creek bottom alongside a series of waterfalls. There were signs of beaver along the creek. I circled the marshy area, stopping in the mud where the game trail ran. A fresh set of bear tracks was printed over the older hoof marks of deer and elk.

I dropped my pack and got down on my knees to look at the large pad marks. I had heard that there might be a few grizzlies left in the northern part of these mountains. I found a good front track. The marks of the front claws were close to the toe; the toe prints were separated from one another and on a curved line: a black bear. On a grizzly, the toes touch, in more of a straight line, and the front claws are huge. Just the same, it was a big black bear. I started up the wet trail, anxious to find the next lake before dark.

I came out to the edge of the big lake just at dusk. It was the wildest area I had seen since coming home. In the middle of the mile-long lake stood a tiny, rocky island decorated with a few scrawny trees. One of these trees was on fire. I tensed and looked around. Who had set the fire? No one had, of course. It had been hit by lightning during the afternoon thunderstorm. I took it as a sign: my burning bush.

The small tree smoked away as I dug out my tent and poncho, preparing a shelter next to a large rock where I could put my fire pit. I carefully picked out all the small rocks and pebbles from under the tent. This would be a good camp, my base camp for the next two or three weeks—until my food ran out or I got sick of trout.

I lit a fire of pine, which sputtered and threw sparks and debris into the darkness. I felt the best that I had felt in months. The light of the fire shimmered off the huge quartz monzonite boulder. It must have been stranded after the most recent advance of the glaciers.

I did not want to go to sleep. Instead, I stoked the fire and ran through the fishing I would do the next day. In my mind I fished up the creek I had hiked today, casting a fly into each deep eddy. I started halfway down to the next lake and fished up, roll-casting to avoid the brush, exploring each tail-out and run with a number 12 Royal Coachman. I fished all the way back to camp in my imagination. An hour, maybe two, had passed, and I was exhausted. . . .

The next morning a fine drizzle dripped through the trees. I kindled a small blaze with the help of a candle. The smoke rose to the lower branches of the lodgepole and hung there like a blanket in the heavy air. This was the day I had planned to look for the big black bear, following his tracks up the drainage maybe into the next basin. Instead, I tied the poncho above the fire and huddled underneath it. I left the fire only long enough to fill my canteens at the lake and catch a few trout for dinner at the outlet of the creek. At least I was where I wanted to be: in one of the blank spots on my map.

I poked at the fire with a stick, glancing up every so often at the game trail, vaguely hoping someone might show up: a beautiful mountaineer with a pack full of kinky hardware or a Shoshone maiden clad in wet doeskins. Come and dry by my fire. Let's build a sweat lodge. A two-hour fantasy of girl bums followed. The fire had burned out. It was what the grunts in Nam called an ass trance.

Five days later I was still waiting for the rain to stop. Each day I squatted around the campfire squinting into the smoke until midafternoon, when I walked to the creek to catch a dinner. I had no complaint with the diet or the solitude, only the lack of activity. I ached for a chance to explore the hidden lakes and basins. By the seventh day I was thoroughly bored. The drizzle continued, never really raining and never stopping for more than a few minutes. Far off to the east I could see the clouds breaking up. The weather there had to be part of a local pattern, with heavy clouds hanging around the crest of the range. At this rate, the rain might last all summer.

I did not have real rain gear, so I wrapped myself in a wool sweater and a windbreaker, stuck a bag of waterproof matches in my pocket, strapped on my Ruger .357, and stepped out into the light rain. A faint game trail led around the rocky edge of the lake and along another creek that tumbled down from the lake above. According to the map it was only a mile to the big cirque at the head of the drainage. Above that, there would be impenetrable cliffs and narrow passes filled with snow.

The rocky game trail dropped down to the creek and paralleled a marshy strip of beaver meadow. In the mud were the day-old tracks of the black bear. I knelt on the trail and measured the bear's rear track with my fingers. The front print was there too, faint but unmistakable. The rain had washed most of the other tracks away; what was left looked as if a human had walked there barefoot. It seemed clear that the bear was headed up the drainage. Maybe he had not liked the smell of my campfire.

A black bear might raid your camp but otherwise presents little danger to human beings. It was too bad that no more grizzlies were left in there. They had been shot out decades ago or poisoned with the predacide 1080. Even a place as big and wild as this had proved too small for them. Grizzlies have enormous ranges: A male in country like this needs 200 or 300 square miles; a female, half of that. In the spring, the big bears ranged from the mountains into ranch country and invariably got blown away.

I found a spruce tree tall enough that I could sit under it. It kept most of the rain off me. I waited, my thoughts drifting. . . .

Later, the wind picked up, driving rain through my light windbreaker. Chilled, I moved up the animal trail along the creek, finding more prints of the black bear. I struggled up a steep grade over a lip of bedrock and found myself looking out over a large lake filling a mountain cirque. Above me everything was in a cloud. The wind whipped the rain into squalls and froze it into sleet. I was cold but wanted to try the lake waters with my fly rod before I left.

I stuck the pack rod together with numb fingers, then quickly tied on a brown-hackled wet fly—one of my dad's experimental patterns—which I cast between gusts of wind. Immediately, I was struck by a fifteen-inch golden trout. I reeled it in fast, too cold to think of sport. I released the fish, a fat golden showing a trace of hybridization with rainbow. I tried another fly: nothing doing. I tied the scraggly brown hackle back onto the line and threw it out into the lake. Before I had time to retrieve the brown nymph, I was hit again by an even larger fish. I forgot about the cold, and I played the pound-and-a-half fish for a few minutes before I let it go. This had been the best trout fishing I had yet seen up here. This high basin must be loaded with game, I thought. In addition to the black bear, I had seen signs of lots of deer and elk on the way up. But that was for another day: I was cold and it was sleeting. I wanted to drop down out of this cloud and build a fire. My fingers were no longer functioning.

Several soggy days later I was on my way out, beaten down by the unceasing rain. Toward evening I stepped out into the meadow next to which my Jeep was parked. I dumped my pack on the hood and inspected the damage that the curious range cattle had done. They had stomped a ring in the duff around it and chewed off its plastic directional signals. The Jeep started right up and lurched down the rutted Forest Service trail, finally joining a graded ranch road. I hit U.S. 287 and turned back toward Lander to gas up and buy a few supplies—including a jug of tequila. ❧

SINGING IN HIGH PLACES

Mark Spragg is a native Wyomingite whose evocative, passionate description of the effects of life "at altitude" brings a level of personal description to mountain writing rarely attempted by earlier generations. His celebration of the feel and excitement of the high country atmosphere reminds me of something Mark Twain once said about the air in the high Sierra, that "it is very pure and fine, bracing and delicious. And shouldn't it be?—it is the same the angels breathe." —P. S.

At Altitude by
MARK SPRAGG

I have always lived at altitude. My bones, long muscles, lung capacity came to be me at 7,000 feet—at a place fallen east and slightly off the Yellowstone Plateau. I think that children who grow at high places are raised more by altitude than by their parents. I think the higher the home, the less we are body, the more we are spirit, and that our structure—gross and ethereal—benefits from the tutelage of a voice that does not speak our language, precisely, that the veil is dropped from the earth's face and she speaks to us plainly, to each atom, insuring that absolutely nothing is lost in the translation, at high places, where the air is thin and her voice freed to melody.

When my skin was broken—and boys often break their skin—I bled oxygen-starved blood, blood anxious to escape the body, blood anxious for a breath of light air. I remember watching it flow from me, drip onto an escarpment, onto steep rock where it blossomed like rare, bright lichen: a fine, tenor blood eager for a choir, to make itself heard to other ears pressed to high places thousands of miles from the pale body who lost it. My body owned a separate language, a harmony of blood and fire.

There are people of the mountains. There are people whose blood sings the same song. I recognize them—my clan—in foreign cities, in other hemispheres, past differences of color and language, we nod, we smile and our faces relax to the reflection of one another. I have sat in a cafe, my eyes closed, my back to a man I've never met and listened to him sing the song his body learned early, and known him for a brother. We were branded in our cribs by the lullaby of altitude.

The angels who sing at high places sing differently, because at high places they are accustomed to the whims of their magic being obeyed. Above timberline their smiles spread slopes of wind-flowers, opening wildly in August, the colors as bright as raptor's screams, in air so moistureless, of such clarity, that the scent of them moves miles along a breeze as though on the naked shoulders of a smooth woman, and the murmur of their petals rises thousands of feet and echoes in the mouths of marmot's dens. These are items my blood knows for fact. I am not courting insanity, or even, lightheadedness. I am telling you the truth, am reading from the text of me.

Once, when a boy, I slept out at 10,000 feet, the air crackling in starlight, and the crimson skirts of the northern lights billowed above me. They folded and refolded violet and crimson and coal, these skirts, moving a moment after the goddess who danced inside them. My vision was perfect. I saw her make her dance. What little water there was in the air had frozen and dropped and shattered along a slide of broken granite, and I looked upward eternally, up the red skirts of Mary? of Kali?, the starlight catching in the hair of her unshaven legs as she danced into me the understanding that the nature of the night is feminine: nurturing and terrible. At altitude, if the watcher is squeezed too closely to the night's breasts, so is his life, held there and lost.

What else do I know? I know that the record of every inhalation and exhalation breathed by any creature who once unfurled a life upon this planet is stored in the earth's mountain libraries, carried there, constantly circulated by the winds that will not tolerate our segregation. Winds of birth, death, of the passion we inspire between them. In these libraries of basalt and gold and shale rub the thoughts of poets, dinosaurs, kings, and children dying young, before they could form words of gratitude or complaint, before they could reckon any difference between beast and scientist.

There are places in the Absarokas, in the Gallatins, where the sweat of southern tribes has been shaken from brown faces and chests and risen north and been rained against a weathered slope; collected there. The speech of whales, of penguins stipples the surface of Montana lakes, and lightning snaps it solidly home. The morning dew of Amazonia collects into the air and separates and beads again on my summer forearms out at work in the mountains, and if I look closely at the reflections in those convex surfaces I may see a jaguar yawn and loll asleep in the limbs of some exotic tree. What I am saying is that the backs of mountains are the spines of books, of entrance to all the earth knows, every minutiae of her history.

These are the secrets ignited by the friction of my feet on earth at high places. These are the secrets I whisper to the woman I love while she sleeps. I whisper what I know; the few things I suspect. She prefers me quiet when we are awake, but I am by nature a talker; my soul finding peace in the rhythms of careful speech.

When we sleep out I sing into the perfect curve of her ear a song I learned as a boy, the song of crystal, the song of stone, and she turns in her sleep, her soft skin rubbed against this range of floated granite, tidal, unhurried range of mountain on which her restless body turns: the sound of crystal getting into her—crystal suspended like plankton in this current of rock—slower than glaciers, formed in fire.

This last summer, past the winter solstice in the Andes—all mountains connected and unconcerned with season—we walked, this woman and I, to a lake at 8,000 feet in the northern Rockies. We camped by its shore, and knew it for a magic spot: it was high enough, this small, deep lake. It collected the seep of its whole, high cirque and across its dark surface, as black and emerald as a magpie's tail, glittered music played in the streets of Cuzco, flute music danced north.

Around us rose granite another thousand feet, jagged against the sky like broken shards of god pottery, when gods stopped at this planet to sip cool water, before my ancestors walked this, or any continent.

Coyotes chorused as we cooked our dinner, their music turned by rock walls back over them, exciting them to frenzy, like some hillbilly band to happiness. It made us smile at their sheer joy, and that is how we went to sleep; in each other's arms and smiling.

I woke in the night and watched this woman up and naked in the moon. She had dropped her clothes by a weather-stunted pine and turned slowly, her arms outstretched and raised, and seemed to be growing larger with each turn; dancing. She then lowered herself to her knees and swept her arms over the ground, smoothing the raised puzzle of tunnels left by moles, her breasts swinging freely as she worked, the moon working along her back, caught in the small of it and in her hair hung around her face. She bent further and sniffed the ground and when I asked her if she kissed it, said, "Of course," and sat cross-legged and stared at me.

I walked to her and kneeled and kissed her eyes and knees and felt the night-coolness rise against my cheek from the dark tangle of shadows held between her legs. It was a rare night of warmth without insects. There had been a week of deep frosts that had worked a plague at them, and for the few left we offered our smoke-soaked skins from the dinner's fire. We took each other's hands and prayed earnestly to stay alive. We had come so high, there was so much available that if we stumbled there was far to fall.

We oddly knew, spoke aloud, that if the single howl of a single wolf were to pierce our bodies—regardless of our precautions, our intent—a child would be conceived, we its guardians, and that such a child struck from flint pushed so close to the moon would be a magic thing, but that not all alchemy transforms us lovely.

We held each other tighter and prayed for beauty. Prayed clearly enough for the song to carry, aware that some sorcery, like an unbalanced genius, spins cyclonic in our souls, twisting us to commonness, sucking song away, dropping us to silence, dropping even mountains into the earth. We sang to the limit of our voices, arching our bodies in the melody we knew. We sang the peaks into the sky and held them there in song.

We pressed our hearts against each other clean, away from fear, away from falling, aware that it is fear that pries loose our grip, and sang out our joy, perhaps simply, because we had risen above so much low country we expected to live forever. We sang the song for every man and woman of altitude; other voices balanced upon scraps of flotsam, climbed atop derelict machinery, on the bodies of their fallen loved ones, but each voice reaching up for joy, for the clarity to dance with angels, to grip the hem of the night's skirts and be flung away into the waiting arms of their extended humanity, and once there, sing. ❧

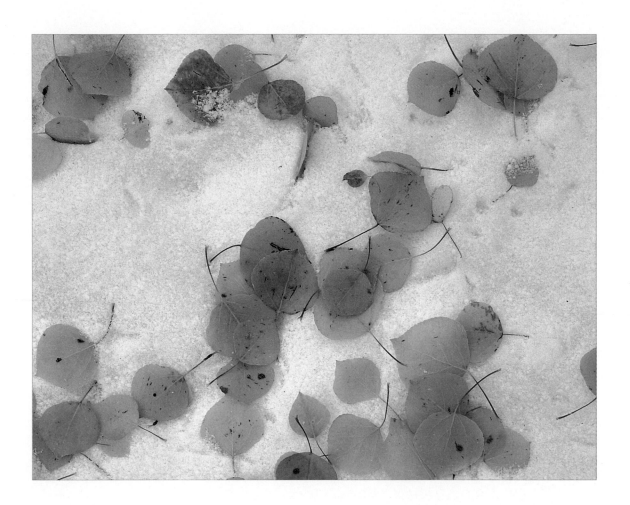

THE CRAZY QUEST

I lived for a few years in a Montana town near the Crazy Mountains, and never got used to them there, off in the distance. They seemed enormously changeable; some days they towered twice as high on the horizon, other days they drifted back to a great hazy distance.

Ruth Rudner has written many essays and several excellent books about life in the high West, and in this story she does what I have yet to get around to: actually climbs up there and gets to know the Crazies from the inside. I still intend to make that trip, and when I do I hope to find as much as she did.—P. S.

Excerpts from *Greetings from Wisdom, Montana* by

RUTH RUDNER

They say the Crazy Mountains got their name when a woman whose husband and son were lost there went crazy looking for them. There are a few variations on that story, but they all add up to a woman going crazy. Crazy Mountains. Somewhere else in Montana, I came upon Crazy Woman Creek. There must be lots of crazy women here. Or maybe they're just more straightforward about it in Montana. Maybe a crazy woman is more noticeable in all this space, like some raging wind that sweeps across the prairies with nothing anywhere to stop it until it crashes up against the mountains. Here, tormented by the impasse, it knocks itself out or pours up the mountainsides to whirl about the peaks in all directions at once, or funnels into canyons or scours valleys. Maybe a woman out here is like the wind, coming and going as nature wills, carrying in her always the power to purify the air, rout extremes of cold and heat, gentle the earth . . . or destroy it. It's no wonder women go crazy out here, living like the wind.

The Crazy Mountains, before their name, were formed as a volcanic dike system radiating out from a central core. A range of high, rocky, knife-edge mountains, they stand there, on the edge of the prairie, apart from all the rest, as if they had nothing to do with other mountains. From their heights you look west to all the mountains of Montana or east to the vast prairie, immense, silent, stretching like some golden sea to the edge of the world. That's all there is to earth—the Crazy Mountains where you stand, the western mountains and the prairie, and, somewhere beyond the prairie's far side, the ocean. Some say other land lies on the far side of the prairie: rolling farmland and city land and ancient mountains and highways running all the way across to the ocean. But when you stand on top of the Crazies, you know you can see the whole of the earth, and you see there's no space on it for anything that doesn't equal the grandeur of the mountains and the prairie.

It was the Crazies that brought me to Montana in the first place. In 1982, a man I met at six in the morning in a cafe in Pinedale, Wyoming, told me he had just come from there. At six in the morning a few locals gather in every cafe in America. They come daily and, daily, the waitress sets down coffee before them without asking. If there are strangers present as well, the strangers have in common that fact that they are strangers. This constitutes an introduction.

I was on my way into the Wind River Range.

"I just came from the Crazy Mountains," the man said.

I had never heard of them. "Where are they?" I asked.

"Montana. My brother and I spent a week there. Beautiful. Those mountains are beautiful. . . ." His voice trailed off. He looked as if he could see them. "Beautiful," he repeated.

"Are there grizzly bears?" I asked.

"No grizzlies. Just those mountains like a jewel."

In 1858 the Crow Chief Plenty Coups went into the Crazies on a vision quest. Except he wasn't a chief then but a ten-year-old boy. When he came out he told his people that the buffalo would disappear from the plains, that a race of white men was coming.

At that time the only white men in the region were a few scattered trappers living more or less like Indians, moving from place to place, leaving no permanent structures behind; nothing to mark their passing but a race of half-breed children and the opening of the West. It was not until gold was discovered in 1863 that they came in droves and built towns. Two decades later the buffalo disappeared from the plains, the white man having managed to do in his brief time in the West what the Indians, on their own, had not done in their entire history.

After I heard about the Crazies, I knew I would come to Montana.

At first I just wanted to be in the Crazies. But now that I'd been in them, what I wanted was a peak. Crazy Peak. Eleven thousand, two hundred and nine feet, according to the U.S. Geological Survey. The highest in the range. Chief Plenty Coups said he'd gone to the highest peak.

Bruce and I went there at the end of August. It was late in the day when we reached the trailhead. The sun was already low, lying on the sky in the long Montana dusk.

On the trail between the trees, the darkness came sooner than I thought it would. When it became apparent we would be caught by night, Bruce went ahead to find a campsite before complete dark. I welcomed his going ahead, welcomed the chance to walk here alone. I maintained a good pace at first, with the last vestiges of light, then picked my way among the stones that held some light, thinking how often in Montana I seemed to hike by night. The night wrapped me like a shawl, warm and soft. Nothing in the night could harm me. I was happy walking through it, although occasionally concerned I might miss the turnoff, which is not particularly well marked. There were no sounds. Nothing moved. I moved. Nothing else. Bruce must be very far ahead. He walks so quickly. It doesn't matter to him whether it's day or night. His feet are as sure either way. I wondered if I'd passed the turnoff. It seemed as if I'd been walking a long time. Two miles surely. Five perhaps. I can lie down, I thought, when I come to a meadow. Lie down and wait until morning. A small fire flared in a large black space to my right. Bruce. I crossed the clear, black space.

"I thought we should stop," he said.

We put up the tent and crawled in, hardly speaking. We had been fighting earlier in the day. I don't remember what the fight was about. I don't really remember what any of them were about. They happened all the time now. He had moved to Bozeman, and we no longer had anything in common except the mountains and our love.

In the morning we found the turnoff near the clearing, made our way across Big Timber Creek a few feet down the path, then continued down, the long descent like Alice's fall into Wonderland, revealing at its bottom Blue Lake, the mountains surrounding it, Crazy Peak to the south. Around the lake, and along the creek running down to it from Granite Lake, a few minutes' walk higher up, were many boulder-strewn, sandy sites to camp. Renewed by morning and the walk, the lingering unease between us submerged itself beneath the smell of morning and the hope of day. We made camp and climbed up into Pear Lake, laying between us and Crazy Peak. Crazy Peak itself we saved for the next day, the day we would have an early start at it, the day we would devote fully to it. Scrambling over rocks on the way to Druckmiller Lake, we could clearly see the route up the southwest side of Crazy Peak, a long one over a broad, high, rubbly boulder field to the ridge, then a scramble over rock to the top.

Now that I stood before it, did I long for it still, or dread it? Was it possible that even toward this mountain I knew I wanted I was ambivalent? How was it possible to fear so much those things I wanted? Why could I not be so single-mindedly bent on my quest, as Plenty Coups had been, that the mountain was only incidental, a means to a dream? But the mountain *was* the quest. . . . The mountain was not incidental. Watching it, I wondered if there was anything on earth of which I was not afraid. What flaw was it in me that led me to mountains, to a world where I must deal constantly with my fears, rather than one that might have been at least a little easier? Wouldn't it be nice if *something* wasn't a test? I try to imagine what it might be like, but come up empty every time. There is nothing else for me to do. Sometimes I avoid mountains, but those are the times they are most absolutely with me.

It was a gray dawn. Crazy Peak stood darker than the dawn, a harder gray against the gray sky. There were no sounds from the other campsites. We ate and started out, heading straight up the steep boulder slope on the lake's south-western side. There was no beginning, no chance to get my muscles moving. It was not possible to ease onto the mountain. It was simply steep, the earth slippery, the rocks loose, the footing unstable. Bruce, who had climbed the mountain once before, slowed himself so I would not lose sight of him. He could have run up that slope.

I picked my way uneasily among the loose rocks. I hate loose rocks. The mixed earth and rock became less steep; became entirely rock, thousands of years of rock piled upon rock. Traversing the slope, we angled continually up. The sky darkened further. Rain would come. Lightning might come. The mountain was entirely open, exposed everywhere to light-ning. On the ridge we would be the highest things around. The ridge was no longer far above us. Getting there would be easier than the first part of the climb, and climbing up the ridge to the peak easier yet.

"We have to turn back," Bruce said. "It's going to storm."

The mountain had been taken from me. It was not my fault. It was my fault. If I could have gone faster, we would have been there. But I couldn't go faster.

"You could have made it," I said.

"I might have been caught on the ridge or the peak. It's probably good luck I have to turn around."

Disappointment, failure, annoyance, relief . . . and renewed longing, because I had not yet got it. When I do, then what?

We walked straight down from where we were, now following our route of the day before from the lakes. That seemed to me a better way to go up. When I come again, it's the way I will start. I got off too shakily on that steep slope. From breakfast to a steep, loose slope. That's the wrong morning for me. Some people get up in the morning and go out and do a thing they've never done. I start slow. I need to work my way around the thing. I need to surround myself with it and enter it and then begin. This, of course, makes me totally unfit for expedition work, but then I would never have been physically strong enough for that anyway. My own mountains in my own time. That's not failure. It's a personal quirk. Why doesn't this make me feel any better?

I fumbled my way down after Bruce, seething. Once again I had proven myself inept, unskilled, slow, ponderous, when in my soul I would dance up mountains. Why is there so much distance between my body and my soul?

It was sprinkling as we reached camp. Within an hour the rain began in earnest. We huddled in the tent reading Hem-ingway. *The Snows of Kilimanjaro.* Harry lies on his cot, dying. No, Harry lies on his cot finally understanding that "now he would never write the things that he had saved to write until he knew enough to write them well. Well, he would not have to fail at trying to write them either. Maybe you could never write them, and that was why you put them off and delayed the starting."

It had been a long time since I had written anything. How did it happen that just this book was on this trip? Bruce had brought it, not I. I had not read Hemingway since college. Even in Paris I had not read Hemingway. Crazy Peak had given me time to read what I once thought was merely great writing, but what I now saw was truth. About writing. About climbing mountains. There wasn't much difference between the two. Sometimes you make it. Sometimes you don't.

The hard earth would not absorb the rain. The water pooled and ran in rivulets, now entering the tent. Bruce crawled out to scour out a shallow ditch around the tent. At once the ditch filled with water which itself poured out in wider rivulets. He crawled out again and deepened the trench. The rain continued.

We read *A Clean, Well-Lighted Place*. When I read that one in college, there had seemed to me to be a place where it was not clear which of the two waiters was speaking. It seemed necessary to me that it be clear. So I wrote to Hemingway and told him I didn't think it was clear. He wrote back and said, "It's perfectly clear to me." I showed the note to my English teacher, who asked if he could have it. I gave it to him. It never occurred to me it might one day be extraordinary to have a note from Hemingway. Not that I'm sorry I gave him the note. He's a poet and poets require talismans. I hope he still has it. But I hadn't read the story since then. Now, as I read it, I could not find the exchange that had been unclear to me. I guess Hemingway was right.

The rain lifted toward evening, although the sky remained gray, as if the rain was not yet finished. Bruce was able to get a fire going (Bruce is always able to get a fire going), and we sat near it, eating dinner, when suddenly the whole top of Crazy Peak lit up fiery red, as if fire was inside radiating out, a brilliant red, rose light, some sacred luminescence. Aware, in the same instant, that it was not the mountain but the sun that made the light, we turned to see the sun behind us exactly at the moment it exploded in a million bursts of flame as if this was the end of the sun forever: one last, effervescent, squalling, bursting eruption of fire. Light now would be gone from the earth.

The sun was gone. The gray clouds folded in on it. The glow left Crazy Peak. We had been given a gift of Crazy Peak we would never had had on its summit. Anyone can climb a mountain, but miracles are rare. We did not speak. We understood that although we were losing one another, we had shared a miracle. We would not lose the bond of our souls, blessed by all the fire and glory of heaven and the earth. ✳

In the Shadow of the Peaks

I first got to know Harry Middleton and his vivid, energetic prose ten years ago when I was an editor at Country Journal. *Middleton was also an editor, at* Southern Living, *but his heart was in the books he wrote about mountains and trout streams, which received many literary awards. Writing up to his death, in 1993, Middleton's last book was written in the middle of the night, after a day of stocking grocery store shelves and a shift on a local garbage truck. His life had slipped into an oppressive grind that must have contributed to his early death. But Middleton left more than most of us get to: some of the most powerful, evocative prose American wild places have ever inspired. —P. S.*

Excerpts from *On the Spine of Time* by
Harry Middleton

In the mountains experience is as rich in vital nutrition as chili and sourdough bread. Sometimes I have lived for days on the energy generated by experience. It is filling and satisfying and lingers in every cell. A scientist who keeps track of such things says that each second of our lives we are bombarded by at least 100,000 random impulses of sensory information. A holocaust of electrical information. Against such an onslaught I fumble about desperately like a man who has suddenly lost his sight and is trying to channel the earth—through one less sense.

The mountains dig at my senses, scrape them clean, wash them in cold mountain rivers, and hang them in a mountain wind to dry. Wading in a fine stream, I often try to reduce myself to a cell within its waters, nondescript flotsam riding wildly on the current of time as it spreads without fanfare down through shallow-filled, rocky valleys and finally onto the wide, flat, sunlit sprawl of the piedmont. I let such moments carry me for as long as they can and as far away as they can from that which seems to be doing me so little good—office politics and intrigue, neither of which I excel in, crowds, bad plumbing, polluted water and grimy air, traffic gridlock, the increasingly dreary task of simply making a living instead of living a life. Up in the mountains, I let all this go for a time and let myself drift toward what I like and enjoy rather than what others believe I need. Be it for an hour or a day or a week, when I am in the high country, I give up and give in, glide with slants of light, dream in cool shadows, cast my line after a good fish.

Once on the mountain highway, once the road rises out of these foothills and serpentines about the scalloped slopes of the mountains, things change, sensations change, priorities change. I change. I gather about me only what seems necessary, fundamental; I delight in what is basic—a cool wind; clean, fast water; the smell of sweet earth; a fat trout in deep water. There is an economy and an urgency to life in the mountains, an immediacy that defines exactness, the defined, whatever is confined by rules. In place of life's clutter, there is daylight and dark and everything from joy and exhaustion to fear coloring the light, giving it shape and substance. You take what is given, even the fear—that the next time you climb this way it will all be gone; the mountain will be slag, trees clear-cut, coves developed, valleys bulldozed and seeded with resorts, streams dammed, all of it tragically transmogrified into the bleary, concrete, shopping-mall sameness I fled from, left down in the netherworld of the civilized lowlands.

The fear is real and I fight it with the fly rod which lets me cast beyond the obvious. Using the fly rod demands a discipline that insists that while on the stream great blocks of life, of time in motion, be allowed to slip by, almost unnoticed. My mind acts in much the same way, casting only to what seems interesting and promising, encouraging me to deal with the small, with currents and eddies and seeps, rather than the enormity of tidal waves. The idea is to concentrate on living rather than merely surviving. The brain is clever and full of cunning defenses, yet for all its splendor and evolutionary magnificence, it leaves me, in some ways, less than the trout which knows its world so thoroughly, so completely, seeing and feeling always the whole, while I feast on scraps of rising sun and setting moon, basins of fissured stone, endless slivers of changing light. When I cast to a trout, there is always that feeling, just below the skin, that I might somehow reach just beyond the given, and feel on my line the full weight of things—the weight of mountain and river laced into flesh and bone by a rising trout.

Below my second-story window, at the edge of the gorge, wild dogwood trees have dropped their faded white blooms. The ground beneath the trees looks like a milky reflection of the night sky, the spent blooms looking like distant points of hazy starlight until the wind stirs and sets everything adrift again. More illusion, harmless, innocent. The earth thrives on it. It's all catch me if you can; now you see me now you don't. Stability is a ruse. Even as I sit in this hard-backed chair here at my desk in this house on this Alabama hilltop, I am spinning, drifting, just as the earth, a less-than-average planet, is spinning on its axis and revolving about the sun, which is but a rather average and insignificant star. And the earth and sun are but two motes in a minor solar system in an average galaxy called the Milky Way that is drifting through the

cosmic darkness at 40,000 miles an hour. When last I heard, our galaxy's course was generally east out beyond the stars of the constellation Hercules. As good a direction as any, I suppose.

Meanwhile, I am getting ready to take off in another direction entirely, one closer to home: north and east, up into the spruce-blue haze and fog that shrouds the Smoky Mountains, where I will for a week or so purposely give up chasing time, the futile and exhausting obsession to grasp it, hold it down, mend it to suit me. We give too much of life over to the wasteful chore of trying to undo, resolve, overhaul, resuscitate, and heal what passing time has a habit of leaving on our doorstep. So busy are we with the past, that we never feel or know the present. No wonder the future is always such a cold and ominous surprise. When I go into the mountains I live on mountain time: the warm press of the present splashing against me, filling the narrow river canyons and steep gorges where the swift water sounds like wind through hollow bones and threatens to absorb the very air. When a trout rises there is only a chill on the skin to remind me that time passed at all.

Years ago I spent a fine week hiking and fishing along Forney Creek near Fontana Lake, North Carolina. To reach the mouth of the creek, I rented a boat and made the short run across Fontana Lake and fished the lower portion of the creek. It was early fall, the first cool days of October, and I walked lazily up the trail along the creek, stopping frequently at every inviting stretch of water. By nightfall, I had hiked only as far up the valley as the old logging road where I dropped the backpack and fished the last hour of dim light. I took one small brown trout; the water went opaque, looked as thick and heavy as quicksilver. The wind came up and I reeled in my line, bit off the fly, dried it carefully, groomed it with the diligence of an old cat smoothing out tangled fur.

The wind took on a lasting strength and I shed the waders, unrolled the sleeping bag, and watched ragged clouds, white as eggshell, move quickly across the blackening sky. Barred owls had yet to call from the deep shadows and the only other sound was that of the creek, the gentle slap of water against stone. A vole scuttled through fallen brittle leaves, and I stretched out on the sleeping bag. Overhead, the clouds took on the look of torn rags and the moon was low in the sky. Up on the ridge an owl called, the sound like a low bark that joined with the sound of the creek and produced a new sound, like a symphony of bass drums played softly, a sound that drifted easily on the strong wind and rose quickly up and out of the pinched-in valley.

Twilight: a time for the arrival of cool shadows and familiar feelings, well-worked ideas, which come these days like animals out of the dark. Time raises mountains and attends to their collapse; its teeth marks are in the stone, in the thrust-up, faulted, folded landscape and on me as well. Perhaps that is the ultimate pull of mountains: we share the marks of time. Mountains let go; I hold on, wanting the dance to be everlasting. But the river moves on. There is nothing like a mountain trout stream to undermine whatever new bouquet of trendy neuroses a man might be nursing along.

A few hours more and it will be full daylight. To the east the sky is already luminescent, glowing. I especially like these hours before dawn and have since my years on the Ozark farm with the old men. The farm was in a narrow valley along Starlight Creek. The creek's cold waters were full of trout. Our days began before daylight, the creaking of the cold wooden floors in the soft dark, while from the kitchen downstairs came the smell of hot coffee and sausage and freshly made biscuits. A meal to give the day yet another dimension of character. We would sit at the small, round kitchen table and eat in silence and the sun would finally gain the ridge. Sunlight crept down the hillsides as though it were red-hot, molten iron being poured slowly from a smelter. Often, I would watch the building sunlight from the back porch that had no screen door and where there seemed to always be a cool wind. As the light came over the ridge like a feathering wave, the birds did not sing. Indeed, everything seemed, for an instant, bound by silence, everything but the creek; its waters moved on as always, the sound of mountains being reduced to flecks of stone.

As the years have passed, I've discovered that a good many people find altitude, a rapid ascent of any kind, disagreeable because it upsets their lives, makes them dizzy, light-headed, and giddy—exactly the characteristics of the mountains that I find so pleasing. I have been fortunate and have spent a good deal of time in the mountains, angling and hiking and just sitting along streams, a happy and voluntary exile with time to sort out that which I know from that of which I am only modestly aware. God bless Einstein and the demise of absolute time, the frightening notion of an inflexibly precise universe. ⚘

LOOKOUT POINT

Sigurd Olson, a distinguished conservationist of midcentury America, brought a low-key, modest mood to outdoor writing. In his books about the "canoe country" of the Canadian border country near his Minnesota home, he introduced me to the idea of the small adventure. Even his grand trips through this tough wilderness seemed composed of a series of gentle vignettes, in which the hairy-chestedness of the traditional outdoor story was replaced by calm good judgment, a keen woodsman's savvy, and a sharp eye for the subtleties of the landscape and its inhabitants. He fished, he hunted, he hiked, he canoed prodigious distances, but when you read him, you rarely felt exhausted by the vicarious experience. Instead, he took you along for the peace and beauty he always managed to show you out there. Reading Olson even today, one just settles into the canoe, or into the even pace of the snowshoe trail, and just enjoys the good company.—P. S.

From *Runes of the North* by
SIGURD F. OLSON

When the hunting moon of October first appears, it is big and orange and full of strange excitement. Then it is at its best; later it pales, but those first few moments are moments of glory.

On one such night we decided to climb the high hill north of the town of Ely and there, with miles of wilderness extending toward the east, watch from the first brightening of the sky until the moon was high and full. It was a spur-of-the-moment decision, something unplanned, and the time actually stolen, for there were many other things to do which seemed more vital. Hastily, and almost with a sense of guilt, we donned boots and jackets and drove around the head of the lake to the base of a long ridge beside the Echo Trail, arriving a little breathlessly just before dusk.

The leaves were still in gorgeous color, sheltered maples still flaming, the ground cover a carpet of reds, browns, and yellows, but that evening it was the aspen that were most beautiful of all. As we climbed the slope and threaded our way through the jack pine, we had no hint of what was to come; but, as we emerged on an open shelf two-thirds of the way to the summit, we looked down on a tall stand of aspen in a valley below and in the approaching dusk their color was old gold and peach, a soft diffusion of warmth we had never seen before. So lovely was the sight, we almost forgot the real purpose of our climb and that the steepest part was still to be scaled if we were to see the moon come up. As we climbed, we turned time and again to look below, to bathe our senses in a glow that was already melting into the dark.

We reached the lookout point at last, a bare glaciated knob at the highest and most exposed pinnacle of the ridge. Some hardy maples still held a few brilliant leaves, but a scrub oak in a protected crevice flaunted its mahogany in triumph over the gales. To the south the lake was tinted with the sunset, and beyond were the twinkling lights of town. As dusk descended, the water turned to wine, then to black, and the molten gold below faded into the darkness of the valley. The stage was set and we watched the ridge to the east.

It was then we became conscious of light to the north and within minutes the aurora began to play, first a vague shimmering curtain, faintly tinged with rose and yellow, wavering across the sky. This was something we had not expected, but there it was, an almost hesitant display to be sure, but northern lights just the same. It disappeared as swiftly as it had come and again we watched the horizon to the east for the first telltale brightening. Then in a sudden explosion of color the aurora returned and now there were several drifting curtains, blending and shaking and crossing one another until the entire sky was a confusion of diaphanous veils finally converging until they met in a swirling mass directly overhead. A fitting prelude to the rise of the hunting moon.

Again it was dark, far darker than before. So absorbed had we been in the northern lights, we almost missed the first hint of the moon in the east. Now in a dark notch of the hills had come a change, a barely perceptible one, but as we watched the brightness increased and the notch became plainly outlined. There seemed to be a boiling and stirring of vapors such as one sees at dawn below a falls or rapids.

A slender scimitar of orange sliced through the mist, first only its thin upper edge, then the whole of its rounded rim. The full moon was trembling and pulsating as it pushed and struggled upward and away from the haze which enveloped it. Now it was half, then three-quarters. The mists were subsiding, slipping away from their tenuous hold on the lower rim. At last the moon was free, an oval, glowing ball of orange; the hunting moon of October. ❧

FAVORITE
HIGH
PLACES

Sometimes our greatest challenges and opportunities for appreciating natural beauty are no farther away than our own backyard—as I've discovered on evening treks up Bunsen Peak in Yellowstone Park, my home. "Suddenly everything is wind and space and distance, and I never know where to look first." Each ascent is fueled by my need for a sense of purpose and forces upon me an unavoidable and welcome reminder of what truly matters. —P. S.

A Mountain of My Own by

PAUL SCHULLERY

When people ask you where you live and you tell them Yellowstone, they tend to say something like, "Oh, in West Yellowstone?" which is the little town right outside the west entrance of the park, or "Oh, I was to Gardiner once," which is the little town right outside the north entrance to the park. Some even mention towns surprisingly farther away. So then you have to say, "No, *in* Yellowstone. In the *park*." Because the idea of actually living in the park is apparently so improbable, you find yourself forced to sound as if you're bragging, just to get them to understand. Most of the time I avoid the problem by saying I live in Wyoming.

I have tried hard not to waste this incredible good fortune, and to milk it for at least a few of the countless things that make it so special. On the job or on my own time, I've explored Yellowstone physically, intellectually, and spiritually. Yellowstone taught me to fish (pretty well), hike (passably), ski (poorly), and, most important, to love wild country. In return I've become a passionate defender of the place, partly because anything so magical deserves to endure and partly because I need a lot more time yet to figure out what all it means to me.

Most landscapes are a little overwhelming if we try to embrace them whole, so we tend to focus on special spots, and that is what I've done here: a favored stretch of trout stream, a few handy, well-worn trails, and some high places from which I can look out and consider the rest. Just a few miles south of my home is an 8,500-foot mountain, the core of an extinct volcano. An early park traveler called it Observation Mountain—an uninspired but perfectly accurate name, for my purposes—but then an official government survey party formally named it Bunsen Peak, for Robert Wilhelm Eberhard von Bunsen (of Bunsen burner fame), who was a geologist of some note. Whatever it should be called, with its steep slopes rising to a picturesquely off-center peak, it is all I could ever ask of a mountain, and one of my favorite high places.

My home is at 6,200 feet, higher than all but a few of the mountains east of the Mississippi. But even at that elevation I feel like I'm at the bottom of my landscape; when I step out my door each morning, I am surrounded by mountains much higher. As a matter of habit, ritual, and need, after taking a few steps toward work I stop and look south for just a moment to see how Bunsen is doing. Whether sharply outlined against the morning sky, wreathed in low clouds, or simply invisible behind a curtain of snow, it always seems to be doing just fine.

Beyond that initial impression, I take a second moment to consider its possibilities for me. Even in midwinter, when its trails have been deep in impassable snow for months, I still find myself considering the hike, reminding myself that I've always meant to make the slippery exhausting trudge to the top in winter, and wondering when the trails will finally clear in the spring. It may seem silly that I go through this little mental exercise every morning, but that's the great thing about exercise: once it's a habit, it's automatic, and it does some good.

When spring finally comes (this year I think it happened one day in mid-July; the next day was fall), I always start too soon. One morning during my Bunsen-gazing I decide that the long crescent of the big snowfield I can see near the summit has shrunk enough, and sometime during the day I realize that I've decided to try the trail that evening. A ten-minute drive takes me five miles and 1,000 feet higher, to the trailhead.

The trail climbs right up into the woods, where I wander around looking for my walking stick. The 1988 fires swept over much of Bunsen, providing me with an unlimited supply of sapling-sized dead wood; each summer I go through several sticks. I pick out a likely section, break it to the right length between two bigger trees, and spend the next few hikes getting it into shape—whittling the worst branches off right away, then rubbing the loose bark and rough branch stubs off against bigger trees as I pass. My palm soon shines up the handle end, and just about the time I get really comfortable with it, some other hiker notices it lying there near the trailhead and I have to start work on a new stick. I wonder if people take them home, or just pitch them somewhere. By late summer I'm chucking it pretty far back from the trail so no one will see it, including me; my next hike usually starts with an extended session of stick retrieval.

Then it's up the trail through a burned forest, along the edge of Golden Gate, a raw, orange-and-yellow gorge with the park road skirting the cliff far below on the opposite side. Like the geothermally altered volcanic rock of Yellowstone's Grand Canyon, Golden Gate reminds me of the bright sedimentary slickrock of the Southwest, but the car noise breaks the mood and drives me away and up, through more burned trees, then a patch of green woods, part of the famous "vegetation mosaic" we heard so much about after the fires—a pattern of regrowth of grasses and seedlings between groves of burned-out and standing timber. Here, where the forest canopy still blocks the sunlight, I encounter early warnings of what I'm getting myself into: snowdrifts in the shade, some reaching across the trail. This will only get worse.

The great thing about a trail you use a lot is the familiarity. I can't bring them to mind from a distance, but as I walk along I recognize dozens of specific trees, one with a peculiar twist to its trunk, another chewed bald by porcupines, another familiar just because one evening it sheltered a brood of grouse that performed amazing feats of invisibility as they appeared and disappeared in the undergrowth only a few feet from me. More dozens of root snags, rocks, and bumps in the trail are old friends; at first they demand a continuum of tiny decisions about where my feet will go, until they go the same place every time from force of habit. Hiking a familiar trail is, among other things, an exercise in unanticipated recollection.

I've timed myself enough to know that about twelve minutes after I pick up my stick I will come to the first blind spot, a peculiar little ledge of white rock the trail winds around in a sharp, nervous turn where visibility is down to a few feet. Here I get serious about loud hand-clapping, which is somehow less embarrassing than yelling "Yo, bear!" This trail has been closed now and then because a black or grizzly bear was hanging around, and I'm not shy about making noise, especially when I'm hiking alone. I don't want to surprise a bear, but I'm almost as anxious to make sure I don't run into an elk or moose.

From the ledge the trail levels out briefly in another burned forest, then abruptly climbs over a shady mixture of mud and snow onto the grassy southwestern shoulder of the mountain, giving me a breezy view of the great meadowlands to the south and west, and the distant peaks of the Gallatin Range beyond. I rarely linger here except to catch my breath or cool off in the wind—always aware that the views only get better—before beginning the series of switchbacks that constitutes most of the climb.

After so many trips it annoys me that I still can't remember if there are five, six, or seven of these switchbacks. I always seem to lose count at the north ends, probably because I stop there to gawk at the emerging vista. But it's on the switchbacks that the snow seriously gets in the way, and soon I'm thrashing around in the woods to bypass snowbanks too steep to climb over. Sometimes I get so sidetracked I give up and just grunt straight up through the woods until I come to the next section of the trail. Once I mistook an old elk trail for the real trail and circled far around into a downfall tangle of lodgepole pine before coming out of my hiking haze and realizing this wasn't the way.

The big switchbacks bring me out a couple hundred feet below the summit, on the north side of the peak. The trail gets steeper, winding back and forth across talus slopes. This is the shadowed side of the mountain, so it holds its snow a long time. Now and then there's a glimpse of the top, which bristles with microwave and electrical gear and antennae around a little utility shed—an odd compromise of the mountain's wildness that I've grown completely accepting of after so many trips.

I've finally reached the bottom end of the big snow crescent now. Though my choice of paths could have been wiser. Some days I stupidly clatter right up the loose talus alongside the snowbank, bracing myself as the small slabs of rock twist and slip, applying all manner of unwelcome torque to my ankles. Some days I pioneer my own swtichbacks, stupid versions of the professional ones, slanting gradually back and forth up the perilously loose rock. At my stupidest I go right up the middle of the huge, densely packed snowbank itself, usually following the footprints of some other equally foolhardy hiker, always aware that a slip of my foot would send me tobogganing down into the trees, and that a slip of this long, deep snowbank itself would do a lot worse.

But today, I make it past the crescent without incident. I'm relieved to be on the last few yards of rocky trail, winding between the stunted trees and onto the summit. Suddenly everything is wind and space and distance, and I never know where to look first. As I take my pack off to get my water bottle (and gasp as the wind hits my wet back), I must force myself into another mental gear, out of the climbing mode and into the appreciating one.

For power of view measured per foot of elevation gain, this has to be one of the best investments around. From the trailhead to the top it's only two miles, and a climb of about 1,300 feet, but the rewards are spectacular. The Teton Range pokes well above the horizon ninety miles to the south. The Gallatin Range, with peaks of more than 10,000 feet, is the entire western horizon. The Absaroka Mountain Range runs along the north horizon to the northeast, where it meets the incomparable highlands of the Beartooth Plateau. The scale is biblical.

I come up here a lot because my awareness of what matters needs frequent renewing. The daily booster shots I give my sense of purpose by stopping to look at this mountain from below aren't enough, and it's a little disappointing to know that inspiration this powerful wears off so fast. It makes me wonder if I'm taking it in correctly, if perhaps I hurry too much and don't soak up all the majesty I need to get me through until my next climb. I doubt that I'm getting jaded by having such easy access to so much beauty, because my amazement meter goes off the scale every time I get up here and look around, and because I'm always noticing something new—a little pond tucked in a pocket of woods that I don't remember seeing before, or a possible new route to a trout stream, or just a change in the light that makes some familiar landmark stand out more than usual. I suppose that even in a home this magical I just need a lot of restoratives.

And few things are as restorative as this summit. Standing on the top of the mountain, looking back toward my little village—connecting with the other end of the line of vision I enjoy every day from my door—I am aware of a deep satisfaction of perspective that comes from moving between two places, each of which is endlessly inviting when seen from the other. ❧

NOBLE SUMMIT. BLESSED LIGHT.

I have always thought of John Muir's essays as mighty prose sermons of deep, sonorous resonance and calm assurance. Muir, perhaps more than any other American writer, defined the literary wilderness experience. He lived it, making long arduous hikes to the most remote parts of the Sierra with little gear and less regard for his own comfort. Latter-day scholarly analysts have called him the prophet of a secular religion of wilderness, with his jubilant, even worshipful, celebration of wild country. —P. S.

Excerpts from *The Mountains of California* by

JOHN MUIR

How glorious a greeting the sun gives the mountains! To behold this alone is worth the pains of any excursion a thousand times over. The highest peaks burned like islands in a sea of liquid shade. Then the lower peaks and spires caught the glow, and long lances of light, streaming through many a notch and pass, fell thick on the frozen meadows. The majestic form of Ritter was full in sight, and I pushed rapidly on over rounded rock-bosses and pavements, my iron-shod shoes making a clanking sound, suddenly hushed now and then in rugs of bryanthus, and sedgy lake-margins soft as moss. Here too, in this so-called "land of desolation," I met cassiope, growing in fringes among the battered rocks. Her blossoms had faded long ago, but they were still clinging with happy memories to the evergreen sprays, and still so beautiful as to thrill every fiber of one's being. Winter and summer, you may hear her voice, the low, sweet melody of her purple bells. No evangel among all the mountain plants speaks Nature's love more plainly than cassiope. Where she dwells, the redemption of the coldest solitude is complete. The very rocks and glaciers seem to feel her presence, and become imbued with her own fountain sweetness. All things were warming and awakening. Frozen rills began to flow, the marmots came out of their nests in boulder-piles and climbed sunny rocks to bask, and the dun-headed sparrows were flitting about seeking their breakfasts. The lakes seen from every ridge-top were brilliantly rippled and spangled, shimmering like the thickets of the low dwarf pines. The rocks too, seemed responsive to the vital heat—rock-crystals and snow-crystals thrilling alike. I strode on exhilarated, as if never more to feel fatigue, limbs moving of themselves, every sense unfolding like the thawing flowers, to take part in the new day harmony.

All along my course thus far, excepting when down in the cañons, the landscapes were mostly open to me, and expansive, at least on one side. On the left were the purple plains of Mono, reposing dreamily and warm; on the right, the near peaks springing keenly into the thin sky with more and more impressive sublimity. But these larger views were at length lost. Rugged spurs, and moraines, and huge, projecting buttresses began to shut me in. Every feature became more rigidly alpine, without, however, producing any chilling effect; for going to the mountains is like going home. We always find that the strangest objects in these fountain wilds are in some degree familiar, and we look upon them with a vague sense of having seen them before.

On the southern shore of a frozen lake, I encountered an extensive field of hard, granular snow, up which I scampered in fine tone, intending to follow it to its head, and cross the rocky spur against which it leans, hoping thus to come direct upon the base of the main Ritter peak. The surface was pitted with oval hollows, made by stones and drifted pine-needles that had melted themselves into the mass by the radiation of absorbed sun-heat. These afforded good footholds, but the surface curved more and more steeply at the head, and the pits became shallower and less abundant, until I found myself in danger of being shed off like avalanching snow. I persisted, however, creeping on all fours, and shuffling up the smoothest places on my back, as I had often done on burnished granite, until, after slipping several times, I was compelled to retrace my course to the bottom, and make my way around the west end of the lake, and thence up to the summit of the divide between the head waters of Rush Creek and the northernmost tributaries of the San Joaquin.

Arriving on the summit of this dividing crest, one of the most exciting pieces of pure wilderness was disclosed that I ever discovered in all my mountaineering. There, immediately in front, loomed the majestic mass of Mount Ritter, with a glacier swooping down its face nearly to my feet, then curving westward and pouring its frozen flood into a dark blue lake, whose shores were bounded with precipices of crystalline snow; while a deep chasm drawn between the divide and the glacier separated the massive picture from everything else. I could see only the one sublime mountain, the one glacier, the one lake; the whole veiled with one blue shadow—rock, ice, and water close together without a single leaf or sign of life. After gazing spellbound, I began instinctively to scrutinize every notch and gorge and weathered buttress of the mountain, with reference to making the ascent. The entire front above the glacier appeared as one tremendous precipice, slightly receding at the top, and bristling with spires and pinnacles set above one another in formidable array. Massive lichen-stained battlements stood forward here and there, hacked at the top with angular notches, and separated by frosty gullies and recesses that have been veiled in shadow ever since their creation; while to right and left, as far as I could see, were huge, crumbling buttresses, offering no hope to the climber. The head of the glacier sends up a few finger-like branches through narrow *couloirs*; but these seemed too steep and short to be available, especially as I had no ax with which to cut steps, and the numerous narrow-throated gullies down which stones and snow are avalanched seemed hopelessly steep, besides being interrupted by vertical cliffs; while the whole front was rendered still more terribly forbidding by the chill shadow and the gloomy blackness of the rocks.

Descending the divide in a hesitating mood, I picked my way across the yawning chasm at the foot, and climbed out upon the glacier. There were no meadows now to cheer with their brave colors, nor could I hear the dun-headed sparrows, whose cheery notes so often relieve the silence of our highest mountains. The only sounds were the gurgling of small rills down in the veins and crevasses of the glacier, and now and then the rattling report of falling stones, with the echoes they shot out into the crisp air.

I could not distinctly hope to reach the summit from this side, yet I moved on across the glacier as if driven by fate. Contending with myself, the season is too far spent, I said, and even should I be successful, I might be storm-bound on the mountain; and in the cloud-darkness, with the cliffs and crevasses covered with snow, how could I escape? No; I must wait till next summer. I would only approach the mountain now, and inspect it, creep about its flanks, learn what I could of its history, holding myself ready to flee on the approach of the first storm-cloud. But we little know until tried how much of the uncontrollable there is in us, urging across glaciers and torrents, and up dangerous heights, let the judgment forbid as it may.

I succeeded in gaining the foot of the cliff on the eastern extremity of the glacier, and there discovered the mouth of a narrow avalanche gully, through which I began to climb, intending to follow it as far as possible, and at least obtain some fine wild views for my pains. Its general course is oblique to the plane of the mountain-face, and the metamorphic slates of which the mountain is built are cut by cleavage planes in such a way that they weather off in angular blocks, giving rise to irregular steps that greatly facilitate climbing on the sheer places. I thus made my way into a wilderness of crumbling spires and battlements, built together in bewildering combinations, and gazed in many places with a thin coating of ice, which I had to hammer off with stones. The situation was becoming gradually more perilous; but, having passed several dangerous spots, I dared not think of descending; for, so steep was the entire ascent, one would inevitably fall to the glacier in case a single misstep were made. Knowing, therefore, the tried danger beneath, I became all the more anxious concerning the developments to be made above, and began to be conscious of a vague foreboding of what actually befell: not that I was given to fear, but rather because my instincts, usually so positive and true, seemed vitiated in some way, and were leading me astray. At length, after attaining an elevation of about 12,800 feet, I found myself at the foot of a sheer drop in the bed of the avalanche channel I was tracing, which seemed absolutely to bar further progress. It was only about forty-five or fifty feet high, and somewhat roughened by fissures and projections; but these seemed so slight and insecure, as footholds, that I tried hard to avoid the precipice altogether, by scaling the wall of the channel on either side. But, though less steep, the walls were smoother than the obstructing rock, and repeated efforts only showed that I must either go right ahead or turn back. The tried dangers beneath seemed even greater than that of the cliff in front; therefore, after scanning its face again and again, I began to scale it, picking my holds with intense caution. After gaining a point about halfway to the top, I was suddenly brought to a dead stop, with arms outspread, clinging close to the face of the rock, unable to move hand or foot either up or down. My doom appeared fixed. I *must* fall. There would be a moment of bewilderment, and then a lifeless rumble down the one general precipice to the glacier below.

When this final danger flashed upon me, I became nerve-shaken for the first time since setting foot on the mountains, and my mind seemed to fill with a stifling smoke. But this terrible eclipse lasted only a moment, when life blazed forth again with preternatural clearness. I seemed suddenly to become possessed of a new sense. The other self, bygone experiences, Instinct, or Guardian Angel,—call it what you will,—came forward and assumed control. Then my trembling muscles became firm again, every rift and flaw in the rock was seen as through a microscope, and my limbs moved with a positiveness and precision with which I seemed to have nothing at all to do. Had I been borne aloft upon wings, my deliverance could not have been more complete.

Above this memorable spot, the face of the mountain is still more savagely hacked and torn. It is a maze of yawning chasms and gullies, in the angles of which rise beetling crags and piles of detached boulders that seem to have been gotten ready to be launched below. But the strange influx of strength I had received seemed inexhaustible. I found a way without effort, and soon stood upon the topmost crag in the blessed light.

How truly glorious the landscape circled around this noble summit!—giant mountains, valleys innumerable, glaciers and meadows, rivers and lakes, with the wide blue sky bent tenderly over them all. ❧

About the Photographers and the Photographs

Annette Bottaro-Walklet has lived in Yosemite National Park since 1984. Formerly an assistant manager and staff photographer for the Ansel Adams Gallery, Bottaro-Walklet's work has appeared in a variety of publications and in several national juried exhibits. She leads photography seminars, instructional photo walks through Yosemite, and manages QuietWorks Photography, which features her work and that of her husband, Keith.

> PAGE 90—North Peak at dawn. Sierra Nevada.
> PAGE 98–99—View from Smith Peak. Yosemite N.P.

Gary Braasch has photographed major environmental assignments for *LIFE*, *Audubon*, *Discover*, *Natural History*, and the *New York Times* magazine, and has been published in more than 100 magazines worldwide. Braasch is an active campaigner and contributor to conservation efforts throughout the world. He lives in Nehalem, Oregon.

> PAGE 13—Cascade Mountains.
> PAGE 44–45—Golden Hinde. Vancouver, B.C.
> PAGE 88–89—Cream Lake Area. Olympic N.P.

Kathy Clay has traveled widely throughout the United States capturing America's most spectacular landscapes and wildlands. She has been published in major photographic books including *The Rockies*, *On the Trail of the Desert Wildflower*, *Seasons of the Coyote*, *Shadow of the Salmon*, and *Yellowstone: Land of Fire and Ice*. Clay makes her home in Dubois, Wyoming.

> PAGE 4–5—Cloud-filled valleys. Kingdom Come S.P.

Willard Clay is a former botany professor whose well-known photographs have captured the splendor of much of the United States. Using a large 4x5 format exclusively, he produces razor-sharp images of nature at its finest. His book credits include *Yellowstone: Land of Fire and Ice*, and *Grand Teton: Citadels of Stone*. Clay lives in Ottawa, Illinois.

> PAGE ii–iii—Winter light on Broken Top. Cascade Range.
> PAGE 6—Sunset. Great Smoky Mountains.
> PAGE 16—Clearing morning storm. Gunnison N.F.
> PAGE 36–37—Sunrise on Big Thompson River. Rocky Mountain N.P.
> PAGE 74–75—Sunset on Longs Peak. Rocky Mountain N.P.
> PAGE 84–85—Sunset. Fall Creek Falls S.P.
> PAGE 87—Lichen-covered rocks. Rocky Mountain N.P.

Kathleen Norris Cook is well known for her outstanding images of outdoor subjects, primarily of the western United States. For three consecutive years her work has been selected for display in Kodak's prestigious Professional Photographer's Showcase in the Epcot Center Pavilion. Cook has completed two of her own books, *Exploring Mountain Highways* and *The Million Dollar Highway*, and has contributed to a number of books, including *On the Trail of the Desert Wildflower* and *Women in Wilderness*. Cook makes her home in Colorado.

> PAGE iv—Autumn. Ohio Pass Road. Elk Mountains.
> PAGE 21—Autumn Road. San Juan Mountains.
> PAGE 22–23—Turquoise Lakes Area. San Juan Mountains.
> PAGE 38—Tent at base of Maroon Bells Wilderness Area.
> PAGE 46—Winter aspen. Near McClure Pass, Colorado.
> PAGE 54–55—Red Mountains.
> PAGE 66–67—Maroon Bells Wilderness Area.

Jeff Foott has worked as a cinematographer and still photographer since 1970. He specializes in wildlife and landscape photography and is dedicated to environmental protection. Foott documents wild animals and landscapes in national parks and other wild places. His work has appeared in virtually every major wildlife and nature publication, including *Audubon*, *National Geographic*, *Smithsonian*, and *Natural History*. Foott resides in Jackson, Wyoming.

> PAGE i—Winter storm. Grand Teton N.P.
> PAGE viii—Jasper N.P.
> PAGE 34—Limber pine. Jackson Hole, Wyoming.
> PAGE 35—Snake River. Grand Teton N.P.
> PAGE 43—Meadow and pond. Yosemite N.P.
> PAGE 61—Autumn aspen. Grand Teton N.P.
> PAGE 77—Fall maple leaves. Columbia River Gorge N.S.A.

Michael Frye is a professional photographer specializing in artistic and innovative images of wildlife and the natural landscape. His photographs have been published worldwide and have been included in such prominent publications as *National Wildlife*, *Outdoor Photographer*, National Geographic books, and in Audubon calendars. He lives with his wife, Claudia, and son, Kevin, in Yosemite National Park.

> PAGE 83—Dall sheep rams. Denali N.P.

JC Leacock is a large-format photographer whose images capture the beauty, grandeur, and intimacy of the American landscape. His work has appeared in such publications as *Sierra*, *Wilderness*, *Outside*, and in Audubon calendars, among others. Leacock lives in the mountain town of Nederland, Colorado.

> COVER—Maroon Lake at sunrise.
> PAGE 7—View from Owl's Head Mountain. Groton S.F.
> PAGE 24—Mule's ears in bloom.
> PAGE 25—Mossy campion.
> PAGE 47—Aspen leaves on snow.
> PAGE 48—Western bistort in bloom. La Plata Mountains.
> PAGE 57—Lichen-covered rocks. Snowmass Peak.

Tom and Pat Leeson have been photographing wild places and wildlife as a husband-and-wife team for over twenty years. From their home base in Vancouver, Washington, the Leesons have worked on assignments for the National Geographic Society and National Wildlife Federation, as well as supplying images to *Time*, *LIFE*, *Reader's Digest*, Nike, Inc., and American Airlines. Their images have appeared in such books as *On the Trail of the Desert Wildflower*, *Canyons of Color: Utah's Slickrock Wildlands*, and *Yellowstone: Land of Fire and Ice*.

> PAGE 58—Sunset. N.E. Olympic Peninsula.
> PAGE 71—Vine maples.
> PAGE 72—Bald eagle.
> PAGE 73—Mountain goats.

Londie Padelsky is a professional photographer whose work includes scenic landscapes from much of the western United States, particularly the John Muir Wilderness. Padelsky's images have appeared in *Sunset*, *Sierra*, *Audubon*, *Backpacker*, *Outdoor*, and *Travel Photography*, and have also appeared as fine art prints. She lives in the mountains of the eastern Sierra near the town of Mammoth Lakes, California.

> PAGE 26—Rock Creek Lake, Sierra Nevada.
> PAGE 56—Mountain reflection in small tarn. Sierra Nevada.
> PAGE 62—Beaver pond. Lundy Canyon. Sierra Nevada.
> PAGE 65—Sunset over trees.
> PAGE 68—Moonset over Sierra Nevada.
> PAGE 76—Red huckleberry and fog.
> PAGE 86—Fall leaves surround tree reflection.

Nancy Simmerman has explored the Alaskan wilderness for thirty-five years on foot, skis, sailboat, dogsled, and bush plane. She has photographed two large-format books *ALASKA II* and *Southeast Alaska*, and her images have appeared in *Shadow of the Salmon* and *Women in Wilderness*. She also coauthored the guidebook, *55 Ways to the Wilderness in Southcentral Alaska*. Simmerman lives on Lummi Island, Washington.

> PAGE 33—Great Gorge. Ruth Glacier.

Keith S. Walklet arrived in Yosemite National Park for the winter of 1984 and has lived there ever since, documenting its grand scenes and subtle beauty. He has explored and photographed most of the rest of the continental United States and Alaska as well, and his work has appeared in numerous national publications and was selected for inclusion in *Best of Photography Annual: 1995*.

> PAGE 8—Granite blocks. John Muir Wilderness Area.
> PAGE 14—Bare pines. Afternoon light. Yosemite N.P.
> PAGE 15—Wild iris. Yosemite N.P.
> PAGE 78—McCabe Lake. Yosemite N.P.
> PAGE 95—Sawtooth ridge. Glacial pool. Yosemite N.P.
> PAGE 96–97—Sheep Peak. Yosemite N.P.